Schwerpunktthema Abitur Englisch

Crash

A Film Study

Cornelsen

Schwerpunktthema **Abitur Englisch** · **Crash** · A Film Study

Erarbeitet von
Dr. Paul Maloney, Hildesheim

Verlagsredaktion
Aryane Beaudoin, Dr. Marion Kiffe, Elke Lehmann (Projektleitung)

Technische Umsetzung
krauß-verlagsservice, Ederheim/Hürnheim

Umschlaggestaltung
orangerie grafikdesign, Berlin

1. Auflage, 1. Druck 2017

Alle Drucke dieser Auflage sind inhaltlich unverändert und können im Unterricht nebeneinander verwendet werden.

© 2017 Cornelsen Verlag GmbH, Berlin

Das Werk und seine Teile sind urheberrechtlich geschützt. Jede Nutzung in anderen als den gesetzlich zugelassenen Fällen bedarf der vorherigen schriftlichen Einwilligung des Verlages. Hinweis zu den §§ 46, 52a UrhG: Weder das Werk noch seine Teile dürfen ohne eine solche Einwilligung eingescannt und in ein Netzwerk eingestellt oder sonst öffentlich zugänglich gemacht werden. Dies gilt auch für Intranets von Schulen und sonstigen Bildungseinrichtungen.

Die Webseiten Dritter, deren Internetadressen in diesem Lehrwerk angegeben sind, wurden vor Drucklegung sorgfältig geprüft. Der Verlag übernimmt keine Gewähr für die Aktualität und den Inhalt dieser Seiten oder solcher, die mit ihnen verlinkt sind.

Die Kopiervorlagen dürfen für den eigenen Unterrichtsgebrauch in der jeweils benötigten Anzahl vervielfältigt werden.

Druck: Firmengruppe APPL, aprinta Druck, Wemding

ISBN 978-3-06-035480-1

PEFC zertifiziert
Dieses Produkt stammt aus nachhaltig bewirtschafteten Wäldern und kontrollierten Quellen.
www.pefc.de
PEFC/04-32-0928

CONTENTS

INTRODUCTION			5
PART A	INFORMATION ABOUT THE FILM		6
	A1	Crash	6
	A2	The Plot	6
	A3	Main Characters	7
	A4	Scene Index	7
	A5	Background Information	10
PART B	PRE-VIEWING ACTIVITIES		12
	B1	Examining a Film Poster	12
	B2	Working with the Trailer	12
PART C	WHILE-VIEWING ACTIVITIES		13
	C1	Character Constellations	13
	C2	Focusing on Individual Characters	13
		C2.1 Events in a Character's Life	13
		C2.2 A Closer Look at John Ryan	14
		C2.3 A Closer Look at Tom Hansen	15
		C2.4 A Closer Look at Graham Waters	16
		C2.5 A Closer Look at Cameron Thayer	17
		C2.6 A Closer Look at Anthony	18
	C3	Examining Interpersonal Conflicts	19
	C4	Evaluating Fictional Characters	20
	C5	Analysing Film Stills	21
	C6	The Language of Film	22
PART D	POST-VIEWING ACTIVITIES		23
	D1	Focusing on Key Themes and Issues	23
	D2	Stereotypes, Prejudice and Racism	24
	D3	Paul Haggis and Brendan Fraser on *Crash*	26
	D4	A Film Review	27
	D5	A German Film Review	29

CONTENTS

PART E THE ISSUES BEHIND THE FILM 31
    E1   The Illusion of Security 31
    E2   Responding to Discrimination 34
    E3   Analysing a Cartoon 35
    E4   Race Relations in the Post-Obama Era 36

PART F EXAM PREPARATION – A SELF-TEST 37

PART G FILM STUDIES: EXTRAS 39
    G1   Selected Terms for Film Analysis 39
    G2   Working with a Film Viewing Log 45
    G3   How to Write a Film Review 47
    G4   How to Analyse Film Stills 48

ACKNOWLEDGEMENTS

INTRODUCTION

Dear student,

The feature film *Crash* (German title: *L.A. Crash*) was made in 2004 and released in 2005. The original screenplay was written by Robert Moresco and Paul Haggis, who also directed the film. A low-budget film produced by a small independent studio, *Crash* received mostly positive reviews in the US and won three Academy Awards in 2006 (Best Picture, Best Original Screenplay and Best Film Editing).

Crash is an ensemble film, one in which there are no main characters. Instead, a number of people are shown as they move through their daily lives, interact and reconnect in varying configurations. The story is set in Los Angeles and focuses on 36 hours in the lives of its characters. The figures of the plot are deliberately chosen to present an overview of the contrasting (and often conflicting) ethnic and religious groups (white – African-American – Hispanic – Asian – Muslim) that make Los Angeles a multicultural megacity.

The main themes of the film are racism and prejudice. All of the characters in the film are highly governed by racial consciousness, stereotypes and prejudices. As they 'crash' into each other (both literally and figuratively), the viewer witnesses how prejudice influences their speech, their thinking and their behaviour. We see that the same people who can be arrogant and abusive in one situation are also capable of selfless and humane behaviour in another.

Crash highlights the often tense relationship between the (mainly white) police force and people of colour, regardless of their social standing. As the US enters the post-Obama era and incidents involving police shootings of unarmed black citizens continue to shake American society, it becomes clear that *Crash* has lost none of its relevance. The film will help you to better understand the problems that still beset American society more than sixty years after the rise of the Civil Rights Movement. In addition, as you probe the background of the film, you will gain insight into the social and cultural factors that characterize life in the US today. Finally, you might wish to compare the development of race relations in the US with the present situation in Germany and Europe, as old identities give way to new ones based on shared values instead of shared ethnicity.

Dr. Paul Maloney

6

PART A INFORMATION ABOUT THE FILM

A1 CRASH

Directed by Paul Haggis
Screenplay by Paul Haggis
  Robert Moresco
Starring Chris 'Ludacris' Bridges   Brendan Fraser
  Sandra Bullock   Terrence Howard
  Don Cheadle   Thandie Newton
  Matt Dillon   Michael Peña
  Jennifer Esposito   Ryan Phillippe

Robert Moresco (left) and Paul Haggis (right) at the 78th Academy Awards ceremony in 2006.

A2 THE PLOT

African-American police detective Graham Waters and his Latina colleague Ria are called to a crime scene where a dead body has been found. At the end of the film, the viewer learns that the victim is Waters's younger brother Peter. In retrospect, the film covers the events of the previous 36 hours. Peter and his friend Anthony carjack (i.e. steal) the expensive SUV, a big expensive car, belonging to District Attorney Rick Cabot and his wife Jean. They then run over a Korean man with the stolen SUV. While searching for the stolen vehicle, white police sergeant John Ryan stops a car belonging to African-American film director Cameron Thayer and his wife Christine. Ryan harasses the couple, who were engaged in oral sex while driving, and sexually molests Christine while her husband looks on helplessly. Ryan's colleague Hansen is disgusted by Ryan's behaviour and later asks to be assigned a new partner. Ryan is upset about his father, who is denied adequate treatment under his health insurance plan.

Jean Cabot insists that the locks on their house be changed a second time because she thinks the locksmith they have employed, a Latino named Daniel, is actually a gang member. Iranian-American shopkeeper Farhad and his daughter Dorri buy a gun for self-defence from a firearms dealer. Farhad employs Daniel to fix the lock in his shop, but Daniel tells him that the problem is the door, not the lock. Because of his temper and his limited English skills, Farhad argues with Daniel and refuses to pay him, thinking that he is being cheated. Later, after his shop has been vandalized, he drives in anger to Daniel's house to demand money at gunpoint and accidentally shoots at Daniel's little daughter Lara, who jumped in front of her dad because he had made her believe she is wearing a protective cloak. Not knowing that Dorri bought blanks, i. e. empty bullets, for the pistol, Farhad believes an angel has stopped him from committing a murder.

Officer Ryan and his new partner come to the scene of a serious accident. One of the cars is lying on its roof and leaking gasoline. The driver, Christine Thayer, is trapped inside. Christine does not want Ryan to help her at first, remembering what he had done to her the evening before. Ryan promises not to hurt her, climbs in and rescues her seconds before the car explodes in flames. When Peter and Anthony try to carjack Cameron's SUV, the police intervene. Peter runs off and Cameron defies police orders, while Anthony hides in the car. Officer Hansen, who recognizes Cameron, tries to defuse the situation and spare Cameron any further harassment at the hands of his colleagues. Anthony later carjacks the white van belonging to the Korean man he had run over the day before. When he discovers the van is full of illegal Asian immigrants, he drives it to Chinatown and lets them go, most likely rescuing them from future enslavement. While Peter is walking home alone in a deserted area, he tries to hitchhike a ride and is given a lift by Hansen. When Peter reaches into his pocket to show Hansen his statuette of St Christopher, the saint of travellers, Hansen thinks he is reaching for a gun and shoots him. He then dumps the body on a vacant lot, where it is later identified by Detective Waters, the victim's brother.

Traffic on Hollywood Boulevard, Los Angeles, California

A3 MAIN CHARACTERS

Rick Cabot	L.A. County District Attorney
Jean Cabot	Rick's wife
Maria	Rick and Jean's housekeeper
Daniel Ruiz	locksmith
Lara Ruiz	Daniel's daughter
Graham Waters	police detective
Ria	Graham's colleague and lover
Peter Waters	Graham's brother
Louise Waters	Graham and Peter's mother
Anthony	Peter's friend
John Ryan	police sergeant
Tom Hansen	police officer
Cameron Thayer	film director
Christine Thayer	Cameron's wife
Shaniqua Johnson	health care representative
Farhad Golzari	shopkeeper
Dorri Golzari	Farhad's daughter

A4 SCENE INDEX

Note: The times given for each chapter can vary with different versions of the movie.

Chapter/ Time		Characters/Action
1	0:00:00	Detective Graham Waters and his partner Ria are rear-ended on their way to a murder scene. The Korean driver (Kim Lee; cf. chapter 16) blames Ria for the accident. They start to argue while Waters walks towards the scene of the crime. One of the officers tells Detective Waters that they have found a dead kid. Detective Waters examines the victim's shoe.

8 PART A INFORMATION ABOUT THE FILM

Chapter/ Time	Characters/Action
2 0:04:42	Farhad, a Persian store owner, and his daughter Dorri attempt to buy a gun from Dirk, a firearms dealer. Farhad's difficulty with English and his temper provoke racist remarks from the gun store owner, who refuses to sell him a gun. Fahrhad is escorted out of the store by security. Dorri finally buys a gun and a box of bullets. Anthony and Peter, two young black men, leave a restaurant arguing about racial stereotyping. Minutes later they carjack the vehicle of a wealthy white couple, Rick and Jean Cabot. The thieves drive away with the car. Waters and Ria arrive at another crime scene to investigate a drive-by shooting between two undercover police officers (Conklin/Lewis). The white police officer, Conklin, shot and killed the black driver, Lewis, after the latter allegedly fired a shot at his car.
3 0:11:00	Daniel, a Latino locksmith, changes the locks in the Cabots' house. Jean is upset about the carjacking incident and launches into a racist tirade within earshot of the locksmith. Daniel leaves the keys on the kitchen counter. District attorney Rick Cabot talks to his assistants Karen and Bruce about how the carjacking will affect his chances of re-election.
4 0:14:18	Officer John Ryan talks to Shaniqua Johnson, an insurance representative, on the phone. He tries to get help for his father, who he thinks has been misdiagnosed. Ryan makes a racist comment and offends Johnson, who hangs up on him. Two Asian men make a deal. One of them drives off in a white van (cf. chapter 7). Ryan and his partner Hansen follow a black SUV. Hansen knows it is not the Cabots' stolen car. Ryan still stops the SUV, which belongs to and is driven by television director Cameron Thayer. Thayer's wife Christine is in the passenger seat. Ryan subjects Christine to a humiliating body search. Hansen is disgusted by Ryan's behaviour.
5 0:21:45	The backdoor in Farhad's shop does not close properly. The lock seems to be broken. Farhad puts the gun Dorri bought into the drawer under the cash register. Cameron and Christine argue. Christine becomes angry with her husband because he did not protest while she was being molested by officer Ryan. Daniel comes home and finds his daughter Lara hiding under her bed because she thinks she heard gunshots. He tells her about the fairy who gave him a protective cloak and helps her to put on this invisible cloak. Daniel's pager beeps as he leaves the room.
6 0:28:27	Anthony and Peter listen to hip hop music in the stolen car, talk about hip hop and black activists. Anthony accidentally runs over a Korean man, who gets stuck under the car. They argue about helping him. Hansen requests a transfer from his partner. Dixon, the African-American police chief, explains why he tolerates a racist police officer under his command. Anthony and Peter dump the injured Korean man at the entrance of a hospital and drive away.
7 0:33:23	Daniel replaces the lock in Farhad's store, but points out that the door needs to be replaced. Farhad mistrusts him and calls him a 'cheater'. They argue. Anthony and Peter try to sell the stolen car to Lucien, the owner of a garage where stolen cars are cannibalized for parts, but Lucien refuses. Graham Waters and Ria are making love when his mother phones. Ria is angry at him for his callousness and ignorance. John Ryan looks after his sick father.
8 0:39:13	Farhad's shop has been broken into and vandalized by racists. Rick Cabot and his assistant Karen talk about Conklin, the white police officer who shot Lewis, an African-American colleague. Anthony and Peter talk about a black acquaintance who steals from other African-Americans. Jean Cabot is angry at Maria, her housekeeper, because she did not empty the dishwasher.

PART A   INFORMATION ABOUT THE FILM

Chapter/Time	Characters/Action
	Peter tries to flag down a bus on a city street but is stopped by Anthony, who insists that buses have big windows to humiliate African-American passengers. Cameron's executive producer Fred makes him reshoot a scene because he thinks an African-American character isn't talking 'black' enough.
9 0:44:05	Ryan tries to persuade Shaniqua Johnson to help his father, but his critical remarks on affirmative action (cf. Part A5, p. 10) anger Johnson, who has him expelled from her office. Farhad blames Daniel for the destruction of his store. He phones Daniel's firm to get his name, but the secretary refuses to give it to him. Detective Waters visits his heroin-addicted mother. She begs him to look for his brother. Waters examines the contents of his mother's fridge. Waters tells Ria, who has been waiting in the car, that his mother wasn't in.
10 0:49:53	Christine's attempt to talk to Cameron fails. The man from the insurance company informs Farhad that his insurance doesn't cover the damage to his shop because he didn't replace the door, even though he had been informed by Daniel to do so because it still didn't shut properly. Ryan waits in front of Hansen's car to offer him some advice. Hansen starts his first day in a solo patrol vehicle and is made fun of by his colleagues. Waters and Ria find money in the boot of Lewis's car. Cameron is in deep thoughts. Farhad retrieves Daniel's receipt from the rubbish bin, thus learning his name.
11 0:56:12	Officer Ryan and his new partner Gomez arrive at the scene of a car accident. A car has overturned and is about to burst into flames. As Ryan tries to free the driver, he discovers that it is the same woman (Christine Thayer) he harassed the day before (cf. chapter 4). She does not want him to touch her at first. Ryan struggles to rescue her, finally managing to pull her out of the wreck just in time.
12 1:02:39	Cabot's assistant Flanagan tells Waters that the DA (District Attorney) wants him to incriminate Conklin for shooting Lewis. When Waters balks, Flanagan offers him a promotion and points to his brother's criminal record, which will be ignored if Waters cooperates. Waters tells DA Cabot what he wants to hear (that Conklin shot Lewis because he thought he was just another black drug dealer).
13 1:09:02	Farhad waits in his car in front of Daniel's house. Lara comes home from school. Cameron is sitting in his car when suddenly the door is jerked open. He fights off Anthony and Peter when they try to steal his car. Peter runs away when he sees a police car approaching. Cameron prevents Anthony from driving off by getting into the driver's seat first. Anthony threatens to shoot Cameron, who grabs Anthony's gun. Cameron and Anthony are chased by police cars. Cameron is stopped. He hides the gun and steps out of the car. Cameron gets into a violent argument with armed white police officers. Officer Hansen intervenes on his behalf to defuse the situation. Anthony hides in the car the whole time. Cameron drops Anthony off. He hands him back his gun and calls him 'embarrassing'.
14 1:17:12	Farhad watches in his rearview mirror as Daniel's van arrives. He gets out of his car and accuses Daniel of cheating him. He is about to fire a gun at Daniel. Lara believes she is wearing the impenetrable cloak that protects them both and rushes to her father's aid. Farhad accidentally shoots at Daniel's daughter. Daniel cries out in pain. When he realizes Lara is not dead, he feels her back looking for a wound. Farhad is left standing outside on the street and seems to be confused.

PART A INFORMATION ABOUT THE FILM

Chapter/ Time		Characters/Action
15	1:20:27	Waters brings his mother groceries while she is sleeping. Jean talks to a friend on the phone. Her foot slips on the top step and she tumbles down the stairs. Peter tries to hitch a ride. Ryan drives home in his car. Peter is given a lift by Hansen. Hansen thinks Peter is making fun of him and stops, telling Peter to get out. When Peter reaches into his pocket to show Hansen his statuette of St Christopher, Hansen assumes he is drawing a gun and shoots him. He dumps Peter's body off the road in the Hollywood Hills.
16	1:28:20	The film comes back to the moment when Waters's car is rear-ended (cf. chapter 1). Waters finds out that the dead kid is his brother. Anthony is seen riding a bus, sitting at the window. When he sees the unguarded van of the Korean man he hit the day before (the keys are still in the lock), he gets off the bus. Anthony gets into the van and drives off. Kim Lee (the driver from chapter 1) finds her husband Choi Jin Gui (the injured Korean man from chapter 7) in hospital. He asks her to cash a cheque for him. When Anthony tries to sell the Korean man's van, he discovers that the van is full of smuggled Asian immigrants. Lucien offers Anthony money to keep them. Graham accompanies his mother Louise to the morgue to identify Peter. Dorri, who works there as a forensic pathologist, shows Peter's body to Graham and his mother. Louise breaks down and blames Graham for his brother's death.
17	1:33:56	Farhad tries to explain to Dorri what happened. He thinks Lara is his angel who came to protect him. Dorri slips the gun and the box of blanks into her bag.
18	1:35:39	Jean calls Rick to tell him about her accident, but Rick is too busy to come home. Jean realizes that Maria is the only person who cares for her. Hansen sets fire to his car in an attempt to hide evidence. Ryan comforts his father, who is in pain. Rick Cabot checks the locks in his house, looks out of the window. Lara sleeps in her parents' bed, nestling close to her mother. Daniel stands at the window looking out into the night. Cameron stops to watch the burning car. He joins the African American kids throwing junk into the fire. Christine calls. Graham Waters finds his brother's lucky charm (= statuette of St. Christopher). Anthony drives the immigrants to Chinatown and sets them free. He gives one of them $40 to buy food for the others. Shaniqua Johnson's car is rear-ended. Snow is falling.

A5 BACKGROUND INFORMATION

The film *Crash* is closely connected to everyday life in the US. The following list explains words and references mentioned in the film that you might not otherwise understand.

affirmative action	government measure requiring publicly-supported employers to give preferred treatment to job applicants from underrepresented groups. Those disadvantaged by affirmative action (i.e. white men) often view it as 'reverse discrimination'.
black vote	African-American voters (cf. DA)
blank	kind of bullet that only makes a loud noise without causing any damage
cookie jar	jar in which cookies are kept (and sometimes money is hidden). A person who 'has his hands in the cookie jar' is doing something illegal or dishonest.

Cosby Show	*The Cosby Show* is an American situation comedy, number-one TV show in the 1980s, in which the African-American Huxtables were presented as a model middle-class family.
cracker (sl.)	abusive or slang term for a white person
DA	District Attorney, a United States Attorney or County Attorney (*Staatsanwalt*). In the US district attorneys are elected by popular vote, not appointed as they are in Germany, which is why Rick Cabot worries about the 'black vote'.
dawg (sl.)	slang term for friend, a form of greeting that teenage boys use with each other
Discovery Channel	cable and satellite TV channel that provides non-fiction programmes. Lucien probably refers to *The FBI Files*, a docudrama series that describes actual FBI cases, with dramatic re-enactments and interviews with forensic scientists.
equestrian team	a team that competes in sports done on horseback. Cameron alludes to Christine's elite, privileged background.
frame sb. (sl.)	make somebody appear guilty by manipulating evidence
gangbanger (sl.)	member of a street gang
HMO	health maintenance organization: a kind of health insurance that offers health services for a fixed annual sum. Members are often required to choose a primary care physical (cf. PCP).
homies (sl.)	close friends
honkies (sl.)	white people (derogatory)
Huey Newton, Bobby Seale, Eldridge Cleaver, Fred Hampton	African-American activists of the 1960s
Internal Affairs	organization within the police force that investigates incidents of alleged lawbreaking and professional misconduct by police officers
L.A.P.D.	Los Angeles Police Department
law-and-order vote	conservative voters
Lincoln Navigator	a full-size luxury SUV
minority-owned companies	firms belonging to a member of a minority group (cf. affirmative action)
narc (sl.)	short for narcotics agent: sb. (as a government agent) who investigates narcotics violations
PCP	primary care physician: a doctor who controls access to all medical services. Ryan complains that his father has been misdiagnosed by his PCP, who refuses to refer him to a specialist.
rear-end somebody (sl.)	hit somebody's car from behind
redneck (sl.)	member of the white rural working class
Shaniqua	stereotypical name for an African-American woman from the inner city
shuck'n'jive/(sl.)	term originally used by African-Americans. It refers to the the way black people speak and act in the presence of authority figures, usually to escape punishment.
St Christopher	patron saint of travellers
three-strikes law	law that requires a high penalty for offenders who have already been convicted of two crimes
UCLA	University of California, Los Angeles
wetback (sl.)	illegal Mexican immigrant

PART B   PRE-VIEWING ACTIVITIES

B1 EXAMINING A FILM POSTER

1 **Think:** Look at the poster and describe what kind of film you think *Crash* is. Make notes on elements (film title, photo, colours …) that influence your expectations.

2 **Pair**: Compare expectations with a partner. Discuss the points you don't agree on.

3 **Share**: Link up with another pair. Together, discuss what you think is happening in the scene presented on the poster.

B2 WORKING WITH THE TRAILER

1 Talk about the following points in your class and take notes:

– What is a film trailer?
– Where are trailers usually shown?
– What purpose(s) do trailers serve?
– What is the relationship between a trailer and the feature film it presents?

2 VIEWING Watch the trailer of the film. Compare the impression the trailer conveys with your own expectations.

3 Based on the trailer, which film genre do you think best describes *Crash*: police film, social drama or thriller? Give reasons for your choice.

4 Watch the trailer a second time. Would you be interested in seeing the film? Explain why to your classmates. Try to talk for at least two minutes.

PART C WHILE-VIEWING ACTIVITIES

C1 CHARACTER CONSTELLATIONS

1 Before watching the film, divide your class into six groups. Each group is given one set of characters to make notes on:

Rick Cabot **Jean Cabot**	**Farhad Golzari** **Daniel Ruiz** **Lara Ruiz**	**Anthony** **Peter Waters**
Cameron Thayer **Christine Thayer**	**Officer Ryan** **Officer Hansen**	**Graham Waters** **his mother Louise** **Ria**

2 VIEWING While you are watching the film, make notes on the characters you have been assigned: What does the viewer learn about them, their situation, their behaviour and their relationships to other characters?

3 a On a large sheet of paper (e.g. A3) create a diagram for your characters showing their relationship(s) to each other and any other information you think is relevant.

   b SPEAKING Based on your diagram, prepare and give a presentation introducing your characters to the class. Answer questions the others may have, and add relevant information supplied by others to your diagram.

4 Working together with the other groups, create a poster with a larger diagram showing the relationships and connections of *all* the above characters. Hang the finished poster somewhere where it can be consulted while you are working with the film.

C2 FOCUSING ON INDIVIDUAL CHARACTERS

C2.1 EVENTS IN A CHARACTER'S LIFE

1 For each of the following characters, make a timeline outlining the events they go through in the film.

a Christine Thayer

b Daniel Ruiz

c Farhad Golzari

14 PART C WHILE-VIEWING ACTIVITIES

2 SPEAKING In groups of four, prepare a short TV show segment in which a host interviews Christine, Daniel and Farhad. As the host, prepare a short summary on what happened to them and collect questions to get them talking about how they felt and what their future plans are. As Christine, Daniel or Farhad be prepared to answer questions about how you felt and what your plans for the future are. Conduct and record the interview, then present it to the class.

C2.2 A CLOSER LOOK AT JOHN RYAN

Chapter	Time code	Contents
4	0:14:18 – 0:21:44	Ryan phones Shaniqua Johnson, molests Christine Thayer.
9	0:44:05 – 0:46:17	Ryan asks Shaniqua Johnson for help.
11	0:56:12 – 1:02:38	Ryan saves Christine Thayer's life.

VIEWING Before completing the tasks below, watch the three scenes listed in the table above. Pay special attention to Ryan's behaviour.

Comprehension

1 Outline the information given on Ryan's situation. What does he want to achieve for his father?

Analysis

2 Analyse Ryan's argumentation to get help for his father in the scene from chapter 9. Does he present his case convincingly? Justify your opinion.

3 Compare Ryan's behaviour in the scenes from chapters 4 and 11. Discuss possible reasons for the extreme contrasts in his behaviour.

WRITING A CHARACTER PROFILE

A character profile is a text that summarizes the most important information about a fictional character. It should include the following points:
▶ background information on the character
▶ the role he/she plays in the plot
▶ what we see about this character from their behaviour.

Beyond the Text

4 In all three scenes, Ryan interacts with African-American women. Discuss why he acts the way he does with them.

5 Write a character profile of John Ryan.

C2.3 A CLOSER LOOK AT TOM HANSEN

Chapter	Time code	Contents
4	0:15:20 – 0:21:44	Hansen is witness to Ryan's misconduct.
6	0:31:16 – 0:33:10	Hansen asks for a new partner.
13	1:11:16 – 1:16:11	Hansen intervenes to save Cameron Thayer's life.
15	1:23:51 – 1:28:20	Hansen shoots Peter Waters and leaves his body next to the highway.

VIEWING Before completing the tasks below, watch the four scenes listed in the table above. Pay special attention to Hansen's behaviour.

Comprehension

1 State briefly the main developments in Hansen's behaviour in the four scenes.

Analysis

2 Compare Hansen's behaviour in the scenes from chapers 4 and 13. Analyse the connection.

Beyond the Text

3 Hansen's behaviour has consequences for him and his status within the police force. Comment on these consequences, drawing on your knowledge of other scenes from the film.

4 The death of Peter Waters – a tragic mistake? Discuss.

5 Write a character profile of Tom Hansen (cf. tip box p. 14).

16 PART C WHILE-VIEWING ACTIVITIES

C2.4 A CLOSER LOOK AT GRAHAM WATERS

Chapter	Time code	Contents
7	0:36:19 – 0:37:42	Graham and Ria quarrel.
9	0:47:16 – 0:49:52	Graham visits his mother.
12	1:02:39 – 1:09:01	Graham is put under pressure to incriminate Conklin.
16	1:31:49 – 1:33:56	Graham accompanies his mother to the morgue.

VIEWING Before completing the tasks below, watch the scenes from chapters 7, 9 and 16 listed in the table above. Pay special attention to Waters's behaviour.

Comprehension

1 Describe Graham's relationship with Ria and with his mother Louise.

Analysis

2 Examine the quarrel between Graham and Ria in the scene from chapter 7. Why do they quarrel? What plays a role in their disagreement?

3 Compare what Graham and Peter's mother says about her sons in the scene from chapter 16 with the facts given about them throughout the film. Why do you think Graham doesn't tell her the truth about Peter?

4 **VIEWING** Now watch the scene form chapter 12. Analyse how Graham's skin colour affects his status within the police force.

Beyond the Text

5 Write a character profile of Graham Waters (cf. tip box p. 14).

PART C WHILE-VIEWING ACTIVITIES   **17**

C2.5 A CLOSER LOOK AT CAMERON THAYER

Chapter	Time code	Contents
4	0:16:27 – 0:21:44	Cameron is stopped by the police on his way home.
8	0:42:32 – 0:44:04	Cameron is asked to reshoot a scene because the producer thinks a black character isn't talking 'black' enough.
13	1:11:16 – 1:17:11	When Peter and Anthony try to steal Cameron's car, he defies both the thieves and the police.

VIEWING Before completing the tasks below, watch the scenes from chapters 4 and 8 listed in the table above. Pay special attention to Cameron's behaviour.

Comprehension

1 Describe Cameron's behaviour in the scenes from chapters 4 and 8.

Analysis

2 **a** For each scene, write down the thoughts and feelings that you think are going through Cameron's head.

   b Compare and discuss your ideas with a partner.

   c Compare the two incidents. What do they have in common (from Cameron's point of view)?

3 **VIEWING** Now watch the scene from chapter 13. Compare Cameron's behaviour in this scene with his behaviour in the two previous scenes.

Beyond the Text

4 Discuss possible reasons for the radical change in Cameron's behaviour.

5 Write a character profile of Cameron Thayer (cf. tip box p. 14).

PART C WHILE-VIEWING ACTIVITIES

C2.6 A CLOSER LOOK AT ANTHONY

Chapter	Time code	Contents
2	0:06:33 – 0:08:59	Anthony complains about the bad service in the restaurant they have just left.
6	0:28:27 – 0:31:15	Peter and Anthony are arguing about music when Anthony runs over a Korean man.
8	0:41:34 – 0:42:33	Anthony refuses to take the bus.

VIEWING Before completing the tasks below, watch the three scenes listed in the table above. Pay special attention to Anthony's behavior.

Comprehension

1 Outline Anthony's criticism of the way African Americans are treated in the US.

Analysis

2 Compare Anthony's critical views of American society with his own behaviour.

3 A typical device in drama and film is to pair two characters who form a contrast. Explain ways in which Anthony and Peter might be such a pair.

Beyond the Text

4 At the end of the film, Anthony frees the people from the stolen van and gives them money for food. Discuss possible reasons for his generous behaviour.

5 Write a character profile of Anthony (cf. tip box p. 14).

PART C   WHILE-VIEWING ACTIVITIES   **19**

C3   EXAMINING INTERPERSONAL CONFLICTS

As the title *Crash* suggests, the film shows us people in conflict situations. Four of these conflicted pairs are listed below:

Jean and Rick Cabot

Shaniqua Johnson and John Ryan

Cameron and Christine Thayer

Daniel Ruiz and Farhad Golzari

1   Choose one of the four pairs from above and form a group with other students who have chosen the same characters.

2   Divide the group into two smaller groups (one for each character). Using two separate sheets of paper, make notes explaining the reasons why one character is angry at the other. Write in the first person (cf. Language Help 1).

3   Choose two students from your group to take the parts of the two characters.

4   **SPEAKING** Both characters sit in front of the class. The other students ask them questions to learn about the nature of their conflict and how they feel about it (cf. Language Help 2). The two characters are not allowed to talk to each other, only to respond to the questions they are asked. Repeat for each conflicting pair.

LANGUAGE HELP 1

All I wanted was …
I was very disappointed when …
I expected/didn't expect XY to …
I became very upset when …
I feel that XY doesn't take me seriously …
I don't think I'm being given the respect I deserve.
I did my best to … but the only result was …

LANGUAGE HELP 2

What was the original cause of …?
Can you describe the situation that led to …?
Why do you feel that …?
What do you think he/she should have done?
Who do you blame for …?
How do you feel about … today?
If you could turn the clock back, would you …?

PART C WHILE-VIEWING ACTIVITIES

C4 EVALUATING FICTIONAL CHARACTERS

In real life, a 'sympathetic' person shows empathy and compassion. Fictional characters (e. g. in a novel or film) can be 'sympathetic' or 'unsympathetic' in a different sense of the word. A sympathetic character is one that you are expected to like, while an unsympathetic character is one the reader or audience is intended to dislike. Generally speaking, a sympathetic character is one the reader or viewer identifies with.

TIP

Sympathetic and *unsympathetic* are technical terms for film analysis. When used in a normal daily context, their meanings are quite different:
sympathetic: *verständnisvoll, mitleidig*
unsympathetic: *ohne Mitgefühl, verständnislos*

Be careful! *Sympathetic/unsympathetic* are no translations for German *sympathisch/unsympathisch*:
sympathisch: likable, amiable
unsympathisch: unpleasant, disagreeable

1 **Think:** Fictional characters (e. g. in a novel or film) are often clearly sympathetic or not. Look at the twelve characters in the list below and group them into the three lists.

John Ryan	Jean Cabot	Shaniqua Johnson
Tom Hansen	Cameron Thayer	Farhad Golzari
Graham Waters	Daniel Ruiz	Anthony
Rick Cabot	Christine Thayer	Peter Waters

Sympathetic characters	Neutral characters	Unsympathetic characters
• Graham Waters ✓	• Ria	• John Ryan
• Tom Hansen	• Rick Cabot	• Jean Cabot
• Daniel Ruiz	• Christin Thayer	• Farhad Golzari
		• Shaniqua Johnson
• Anthony		
• Peter Waters		
• Cameron Thayer ✓		

2 **Pair:** Compare your list with a partner.

3 **Share:** SPEAKING Create a short radio report in which you and your partner discuss the characters you disagree on. Discuss the reasons for your choices and the difficulties you may have had in assessing your response to certain characters. Present it to the class.

C5 ANALYSING FILM STILLS

The way we react to a character in a film is influenced by the way this character is visually presented. Our reaction can be influenced by factors such as the position of the character within the frame, the camera angle, the lighting and colours, and the perceived distance between the viewer and the character. (cf. Part G4: How to Analyse Film Stills, p. 48).

A 00:16:45

B 01:02:37

1. For each still, outline the situation briefly.
2. Compare the way John Ryan is presented in the two stills. Use the aspects listed in Part G4 on p. 48 to analyse how the visual presentation of the character influences the viewer's feelings toward him.
3. Choose one of the two stills and write an analysis in which you present your findings from tasks 1 and 2.

C6 THE LANGUAGE OF FILM

Film combines photography, drama, language, music and sound effects to create a unique art form. The interplay of these elements determines how we respond to the film.

VIEWING Watch the scene 1:17:12 – 1:20:18.

Comprehension

1 Outline the events that lead to the conflict between Farhad and Daniel.

Analysis

2 Watch the scene a second time. While you are watching, make notes in the middle column about your emotional response to it.

Action	Your emotional response	Film technique(s)
Farhad waits for Daniel to arrive.		
Lara hears the van and runs to the window.		
Farhad gets out of the car and confronts Daniel. They argue.		
Lara sees her father in danger and runs to help him.		
Lara jumps into Daniel's arms; Farhad fires a shot.		
Daniel carries Lara into the house.		
Farhad is left standing in the street.		

3 Write the film techniques used in the scene in the third column of the table (cf. Part G, pp. 39 ff., if necessary).

4 Examine how the various elements of film-making are employed here to create suspense and to engage the viewer.

PART D POST-VIEWING ACTIVITIES

D1 FOCUSING ON KEY THEMES AND ISSUES

1 a Think: Decide which of the words below are important themes in the film *Crash* and tick (✓) the boxes next to them.

fear		insecurity		race	✓
crime	✓	moral dilemma		aggression	
family ties	✓	discrimination	✓	anger	
cars		isolation		Los Angeles	✓
guns		prejudice	✓	power	

b For each theme you choose, write down in a few sentences how it plays a role in the film.

The movie is about prejudices in a big city where many cultures live together. Because of the diferent race people get discriminate. But the crime plays also a big role in the movie because lots of characters do something iligeal. we also see different families with different family ties, in this movie.

2 a Pair: Compare your choices with a partner. Together, choose the five themes that you think are most important in the film. Make notes on the reasons for your choices.

LANGUAGE HELP
- I'd like to suggest that … / We came up with the following ideas: … / First of all, we thought …
- The topic of … occurs again and again / comes up when …

b Share: Present your choices to the class.

3 WRITING With your partner, write a text for a radio ad for the movie, in which the most important themes are included. Read your ad to the class.

D2 STEREOTYPES, PREJUDICE AND RACISM

The following dialogue is an excerpt from the scene in the gun store (00:04:48 – 00:05:46):

DIRK: You get one free box of ammunition, what kind you want?

FARHAD *(in Farsi)*: What did he say, 'ammunition'?

DORRI *(in Farsi)*: He said, 'What kind of bullets?'

FARHAD *(in Farsi)*: The kind that fit.

DORRI *(in Farsi)*: There's more than one kind.

FARHAD *(in Farsi)*: I don't know anything about guns!

DORRI *(in Farsi)*: Another good reason not to buy one!

FARHAD *(in Farsi)*: Don't start with me again.

DIRK: Yo, Osama, plan the jihad on your own time. What do you want?

FARHAD *(in Farsi)*: What is he saying about jihad? *(to Dirk, in English)*: Are you making insult at me?

DIRK: 'Am I making insult at you?' Is that the closest you can come to English?

FARHAD: Yes, I speak English. I am American citizen!

DIRK: Oh, God, here we go.

FARHAD: I have rights like you! I have right to buy gun!

Dirk pulls the gun back to his side of the counter.

DIRK: Not from my store, you don't. Andy, get him out of here now!

Dirk nods toward the security guard, who heads his way. Dorri sees him coming.

DORRI: Dad, go wait in the car.

DIRK: Now get out!

FARHAD *(to Dirk)*: You are ignorant man!

DIRK: Yeah, I'm ignorant? You're liberating my country and I'm flying 747s into your mud huts and incinerating your friends. Get the fuck out of my store.

FARHAD: No you get the fuck!

SEC. GUARD *(taking his arm)*: Come on!

FARHAD: No, don't touch me! This man cheats me!

DIRK: Get out!

Dirk, Farhad and Dorri at the gun store (00:05:23)

PART D POST-VIEWING ACTIVITIES   **25**

Comprehension

1 Complete the following sentences:

   A Dirk gets impatient when two customers _speaks an different language_.

   B Because of their appearance and language, Dirk concludes that Farhad and Dorri _arent American citizens and they could mean some attac_.

   C When Dirk calls Farhad 'Osama', he means _that he could be a terrorist_.

   D Farhad gets angry because _of Dirks prejudice / he wants to be seen_.

   E Dirk gets angry because _Farhad gets angres a and arrogant_.

Analysis

2 The film *Crash* was made in 2004, only three years after the terrorist attacks on 9/11. Point to places in the text where Dirk alludes to the attacks and the subsequent war against the Taliban in Afghanistan. Analyse the effect they have on his behaviour.

3 Examine Farhad's response to Dirk's aggressiveness. Why does he feel that he is being cheated?

Beyond the Text

4 Read the information box below. Then decide which of the three terms (*stereotype, prejudice, racism*) best describes Dirk's attitude. Discuss.

INFOBOX	Stereotypes, prejudice, racism

The terms *stereotype*, *prejudice* and *racism* are often used to mean the same thing. In sociology however, they each have distinct meanings:
Stereotypes are generalized ideas or opinions about a certain group of people (based on race, nationality, gender, age, ethnicity or sexual orientation) which ignore individual differences. They can focus on almost any aspect (appearance, food preferences, etc.). Stereotypical notions are also referred to as **clichés**.
Prejudice is the judgment or opinion that someone forms about a person before knowing them. The judgement or opinion is based on that person belonging to a certain group.
Racism is prejudice based on a set of beliefs someone has about a certain ethnicity. This prejudice is used to support the belief that one ethnicity is inferior or superior to another.

5 **WRITING** Write an email to Paul Haggis to comment on the following statement he made: '*Crash* is about fear of strangers. It's about how everyone hates to be judged but sees no contradiction in judging others.' Refer also to the examples you have analysed.

PART D POST-VIEWING ACTIVITIES

D3 PAUL HAGGIS AND BRENDAN FRASER ON *CRASH*  SPT354801-01

LISTENING You are going to hear host Neal Conan interview director Paul Haggis and actor Brendan Fraser for his NPR show *Talk of the Nation*. Listen to the interview twice and tick (√) the correct answer for each question. Each number has only one correct answer.

Brendan Fraser, actor in the film *Crash*

1. Which of the following statements does Haggis **not** say about modern society?

   ○ A We only feel safe in our cars.
   ○ B We now feel unsafe in our homes.
   ○ C We are afraid of people we don't know.
   ○ D We only feel something when we bump into other people.

2. Brendan Fraser took the role of District Attorney Rick Cabot because ...

   ○ A he was out of work at the time.
   ○ B his own father had been a district attorney.
   ○ C he had often played similar film roles in the past.
   ○ D he wanted to play a role in a socially relevant film.

3. Fraser says that Cabot is faced with a difficult moral decision and ...

   ○ A doesn't know what to do.
   ○ B makes the wrong decision.
   ○ C has a conflict with his wife for that reason.
   ○ D hands the responsibility down to the people below him.

4. Neal Conan says that, unlike the other film characters, Cabot ...

   ○ A seems very one-sided.
   ○ B has both good and bad sides.
   ○ C knows exactly what he wants.
   ○ D never reveals his true character.

5. While spending time with Los Angeles District Attorney Steve Cooley, Fraser...

   ○ A felt out of place.
   ○ B gained respect for him and his job.
   ○ C learned how to play the role convincingly.
   ○ D saw what really happens behind the scenes.

6. Fraser says that the main topic of the film *Crash* is ...

   ○ A finding who is to blame for ethnic conflicts.
   ○ B finding what direction American society is moving in.
   ○ C understanding the basic values that govern human relations.
   ○ D understanding how people in a multi-ethnic society deal with each other.

D4 A FILM REVIEW

The following review appeared in the British newspaper *The Guardian*:

Caught in the network of fate PHILIP FRENCH

'Nobody touches you ... until you crash into them.'

At the beginning of their classic 1963 sociological work on ethnicity in the United States, *Beyond the Melting Pot*, Nathan Glazer and Daniel Patrick Moynihan wrote: 'The point about the melting pot is that it did not happen. At least not in New York and, mutatis
5 mutandis, in those parts of America which resemble New York.' This is the subject of *Crash*, the debut as writer-director of Paul Haggis, [...] in which the benign notion of America as a melting pot is replaced by the image of a seething cauldron of racial prejudice.

The movie begins at a night-time accident scene in Los Angeles,
10 with an African-American later to be revealed as Graham, a plain-clothes cop (Don Cheadle), saying that in New York City you walk around the city and brush into people, but in Los Angeles you just drive around and nobody touches you. That is until you crash into them. So from the start Los Angeles and crashes are announced as metaphors and reality and the movie
15 proceeds to examine the relationships between a variety of citizens over the previous 36 hours during the run-up to Christmas, supposedly a time of peace and goodwill.

Crash follows the form [...] of presenting city life through a multitude of linked stories in which numerous characters' paths crisscross.
20 Only here there is one obsessive issue – race, as it affects relationships and decisions, shapes and distorts character, and determines social policy. An Iranian shopkeeper, paranoid since the corrosive suspicions following 9/11, buys a gun to protect his store and develops a hatred for a Mexican locksmith. A white District Attorney (Brendan Fraser) and his wife (Sandra
25 Bullock) are car-jacked by two armed blacks. This drives the DA to consider how this affects his re-election campaign and deepens her neurotic alienation from society. An embittered veteran cop (Matt Dillon) viciously harasses a middle-class black couple, driving a wedge between the two, and disgusting his young partner, a recent recruit to the force. A Chinese victim of a
30 hit-and-run accident turns out to be a people-smuggler, transporting Cambodians into bondage. An overzealous undercover cop (white) kills a black colleague, in the belief that he's a drug dealer, and Internal Affairs investigate.

At the centre the plain-clothes cop Graham is having an affair with a
35 Latina colleague, coping with his sick mother, delinquent brother, and a variety of investigations.

In what some may regard as an overly contrived fashion, these stories are neatly dovetailed and interwoven to make ironic and often paradoxical points. Two characters for instance, seemingly drawn together by chance,
40 are in fact mirror images of each other; both carry with them figurines of St Christopher as talismans for their journeys through life. The surface is realistic and the characters neatly sketched, but they are part of a network of

4 *mutatis mutandis* (Latin) making the necessary changes
6 *benign* harmless
7 *seething cauldron* brodelnder Kessel
10 *plain-clothes cop* police officer not wearing a uniform
16 *run-up to sth.* (n) (sl) time before sth.
19 *crisscross* (v) cross more than once
20 *obsessive* forcing you to think about sth.
21 *distort sth.* etw. verbiegen
22 *corrosive* destructive
26–27 *alienation* Entfremdung
27 *vicious* ['vɪʃəs] bösartig
27 *harass sb.* annoy sb. in an extreme way
28 *wedge* Keil
31 *bondage* (fml) enslavement
31 *overzealous* [ˌəʊvəˈzeləs] übereifrig
35 *delinquent* criminal
37 *contrived* konstruiert, unnatürlich
38 *dovetailed/interwoven* linked
40 *figurine* small statue

28 PART D POST-VIEWING ACTIVITIES

→ sometimes good people can be forced into acting badly
→ otherwise bad people acts good and of kindness

fate and destiny that reveals the city and modern life in all its mystery. This is a world where good people can be forced into acting badly, and ostensibly
45 bad people perform acts of kindness and heroism; where the guilty go free and decent men are spurned and punished; where the wise are baffled and the stupid go accidentally to the heart of the matter.

Conclusion

Paul Haggis, who has considerable experience writing for TV, and his co-screenwriter Bobby Moresco, have an acute ear for a variety of speech,
50 and their picture is sharply observed and frequently extremely funny as well as artfully orchestrated. It ends on a tragic note, but they manage to avoid easy cynicism or fashionable despair.

44 *ostensibly* seemingly
46 *spurn sb* reject sb.
46 *baffled* confused
49 *acute* sharp

From: 'Hollywood's Last Taboo', *The Guardian*, 14 August 2005

Comprehension

1. Mark the statement that best summarizes French's opinion of the film:
   A *Crash* shows that no one can escape fate.
   B *Crash* is a cleverly made mixture of comedy and tragedy.
   C *Crash* reveals the ugly reality behind the myth of the melting pot.

2. Divide the text into sections. Give each section a heading and make notes on the most important points.

3. Use your notes from task 2 to write a summary of the text.

Analysis

4. a In the opening paragraph (ll. 1–8), the author contrasts two metaphors, the 'melting pot' and the 'seething cauldron'. Explain the two metaphors.

   b Find other examples of metaphors used by the author and analyse their meaning in context.

Beyond the Text

5. a Film and book reviews often contain words that convey a positive or a negative attitude. In the two word clouds below, you find three examples of each. Add at least four more words from the text to each cloud.

   Cloud 1 (positive): realistic, free, funny, neatly, sketched, protect, decent, acute, kindness, amsterdam, Freuellichly*

   Cloud 2 (negative): prejudice, punished, badly, contrived, cynicism, corrosive

   b **WRITING** Write a short text (150–200 words) in which you express your opinion of the film *Crash*. Justify your opinion using at least five of the words you added to the word clouds in task 5a. Refer to p. 47 in Part G if necessary.

D5 A GERMAN FILM REVIEW

1 **MEDIATION** Your American exchange partner was surprised to learn that the film *Crash* (in Germany: *L.A. Crash*) was only moderately successful in Germany and wants to know why. You find the following review on the internet and summarize the main points for her/him in the form of an email.

Gottes Crashtest-Dummys DANIEL HAAS

Im Fachjargon heißen sie Talking Heads, sprechende Köpfe. Sie kommen immer dann zum Einsatz, wenn ein Film seine Geschichte nicht in Bilder und Handlung übersetzen kann. Dann müssen sie die Story erklären, Referenten des Regisseurs. [...] Viel reden, wenig handeln heißt die Devise, und
5 die Ersetzung der vita activa durch rhetorische Betriebsamkeit wird dann zum buchstäblich vielsagenden Stilprinzip, mit dem sich Figuren und Konflikte entwickeln lassen.

„L.A. Crash", das Regiedebüt des Drehbuchautors Paul Haggis, will jedoch ein Film der urbanen Kollisionen sein, ein Szenario der Zusammen-
10 stöße. Schon das Filmplakat garantiert ein Höchstmaß an Schmerz und Dramatik: Es zeigt einen Mann, der schreiend ein Kind in den Armen hält. Es muss der Moment einer Katastrophe sein, der hier ins Bild gefasst ist, ein Augenblick, in dem Mensch und Schicksal aufeinanderprallen.

Es gibt viele solcher Szenen in Haggis' Film, in denen die Gewalt in das
15 Leben von Menschen einbricht und sie zeichnet: den auf dem Plakat gezeigten mexikanischen Schlosser, auf dessen Tochter geschossen wurde; den afroamerikanischen TV-Produzenten, dessen Freundin vergewaltigt wird; den weißen Staatsanwalt und seine Frau, die von schwarzen Gangstern ausgeraubt werden; den aus [dem] Iran stammenden Ladenbesitzer,
20 der mit der Waffe loszieht, um Vergeltung zu üben.

Dennoch ist das Drama des „Million Dollar Baby"-Autors ein Film der Talking Heads, von Figuren, die wortreich über das Leben räsonieren. Gleich zu Beginn erklärt der schwarze Polizist (Don Cheadle) seiner Kollegin, einer Latina (Jennifer Esposito), dass die Menschen, eingesperrt in ihren Autos,
25 am Leben und an sich selbst vorbeidriften. Nur ein Zusammenstoß könne sie aus diesem Dilemma befreien. Die Kollision als Katastrophe und Katharsis, das ist nicht besonders subtil, und tatsächlich ist „L.A. Crash" in seiner Dramaturgie so plakativ wie ein Thesenpapier. [...]

Auf den ersten Blick scheint der Film ein komplexes Bild gesellschaftli-
30 cher Schuldzusammenhänge zu vermitteln, die der einzelne nicht überschauen kann; ein Panorama, in das der Zufall Menschen mal hierhin, mal dorthin dirigiert und sie wahlweise zu Rettern oder Mördern, Verfolgern oder Erlösern macht. Doch der extreme Realismus der Darstellung, die inszenatorische Härte sind nur ein Bluff: „L. A. Crash" will nicht die neue
35 Unübersichtlichkeit der Schmelztiegelgesellschaft und deren Gefährdungen aufzeigen, sondern eine Utopie bebildern. Die zeigt sich weniger auf der Inhaltsebene der einzelnen Episoden, die exzellent gespielt und in ihrem Naturalismus teilweise erschütternd sind, als in der Struktur des Films.

Paul Haggis, writer/director of the film *Crash*

In Haggis' Welt waltet eine Schicksalssymmetrie, die schließlich allen
den richtigen Platz zuweist. Der Geist, der stets das Böse will, schafft auch
hier das Gute: Der Gangster hat zwar ein Auto geklaut, darin befinden sich
aber die Opfer einer Schlepperbande, die am Ende frei kommen; der rassistische Cop bedrängt eine Unschuldige, rettet sie aber später aus einem
brennenden Auto. Überwölbt von einem sakral wabernden Soundtrack,
macht diese Erzählung deutlich: Mögen Menschen auch in sinnloser Gewalt kollidieren, mögen ihre Handlungen von Gier und Rachsucht bestimmt sein – ein übergeordnete Instanz lenkt alles in einen sinnvollen
Zusammenhang.

Deshalb ist „L. A. Crash" letztlich kein naturalistisches, sondern ein metaphorisches Projekt. Es setzt Figuren als Statthalter für die große amerikanische Hoffnung ein, am Ende doch das große soziale Experiment der
Neuzeit zu sein, in der ein gerechtes Leben über die Grenzen von Hautfarbe
und Herkunft möglich ist. Rassismus und seine gewalttätigen Eruptionen
werden dabei nur vordergründig als Ursachen korrupter Strukturen inszeniert, eigentlich sind sie Fügung. Es ist eine starke, aber auch naive Ethik, zu
der sich Haggis hier aufschwingt.

From: 'Kinodrama "L. A. Crash": Gottes Crashtest-Dummys', *Spiegel Online*,
4 August 2005

WRITING A MEDIATION TEXT

When you do a mediation between speakers of German and English, you have to explain what is written in a text in the other language, and for a specific audience and situation. You do *not* translate a text word for word.
- Start by making notes on the most important information in the text. What is essential for the other person to know?
- Adjust the language, style and register of the text with the situation/person that you are mediating for.
- Give the person the relevant information in an organized manner. Keep in mind cultural aspects that may influence the person's understanding of the text/situation.

PART E   THE ISSUES BEHIND THE FILM

E1   THE ILLUSION OF SECURITY

Handguns and other firearms can be obtained more easily in the US than in many other countries. The following text examines a dilemma that is rapidly becoming a major problem between police officers and (potentially armed) citizens.

When both sides are armed and dangerous   Martin Kaste

The recent targeted attacks on police in Dallas and Baton Rouge have law enforcement on edge. Some departments are telling officers to patrol in pairs when possible, and to be extra vigilant about possible ambush.

Complicating matters is the question of how to interpret and react to the
5 presence of a gun. With more Americans now exercising their legal right to carry firearms, police find themselves having to make rapid judgments about whether an armed citizen is a threat.

While police are more sensitive to the presence of legal guns now, the dilemma isn't a new one. Gun rights groups started a push for more permis-
10 sive laws in the 1990s, and most states now allow concealed carry, open carry or both. [...]

That's one of the challenges for police: Even in states with open carry, when people see someone with a gun, they tend to call the cops — and then the police get the thankless job of challenging someone who may or may not
15 be a threat. One high-ranking officer in Texas calls it a 'headache.'

'When you have all these people running around with guns and rifles, you don't know who the bad guy is,' he says.

Another potential headache is concealed-carry permits, and the people who like to keep their guns secret, like Joseph Olson of Minnesota. [...]
20 Olson says he thought Minnesota police had adapted to the reality of legal guns — until he was pulled over by an especially nervous-seeming cop.

'His voice had a tremor in it and I remember thinking to myself, "Oh, my God." I decided when I heard his voice that I was not going to introduce another element into the transaction,' Olson says. He decided not to
25 mention his gun.

Minnesota law doesn't require people to tell police they have a gun unless asked. Instructors give conflicting advice on this — but cops say they appreciate being told as soon as possible. Most of them have stories about close calls, when a legal gun appeared in the wrong way.
30 One officer recalls telling a gun owner, 'Do you realize you almost died tonight?' The officer, whom we're not identifying because he doesn't have permission from work to talk about this, says he'd pulled the man over for a routine traffic stop.

1 *targeted* gezielt
1–2 *law enforcement* the police
2 *on edge* nervous
3 *vigilant* ['vɪdʒɪlənt] watchful
3 *ambush* surprise attack
9–10 *permissive* liberal
10 *concealed carry* (n.) right to carry a gun that cannot be seen by others
10–11 *open carry* (n) right to carry a gun that can be seen by others
21 *pull sb. over* (infml) stop sb. who is driving a vehicle
22 *tremor* nervous vibration caused by fear
24 *transaction* (fml) business
29 *close call* (infml) situation that nearly ended in disaster

'So I said, "I see you have a permit to carry. Do you have a firearm in the vehicle?"'

'And ... [he said] "Yeah, it's right here," and he reaches over to his passenger seat, and I'm going, "Stop. Don't move," and he grabs this shirt,' the officer recalls. 'And I can then see a gun in it, and he's grabbing it.'

The officer says he managed to grab the man's arm before being forced to pull his own gun, but police have shot motorists for a lot less than that.

Minnesota is an example of a state that's still adjusting to its new gun culture, and the state hasn't introduced any specific training for officers on how best to handle legally armed citizens. Some wonder if that played a role in the death of Philando Castile earlier this month. He's the black man who was shot during a traffic stop; his girlfriend, who was in the car with him, has said he was trying to tell the officer about his permitted gun.

Scott Dibble, a state senator from Minneapolis, says he's surprised officers haven't been given specific training for these situations, and he's also concerned that members of the public aren't being given clear, consistent instructions on how to inform officers that they're armed.

Dibble favors maximum transparency: 'Seems like the right thing to do is to say, "Officer, I'm a concealed-carry permit holder, I have a firearm, I don't want you to be surprised should you see it."'

Then again, Dibble says, that's apparently what Philando Castile was trying to do when he got shot by a police officer.

49 *consistent* einheitlich

From: 'Gun Carry Laws Can Complicate Police Interactions', *NPR Morning Edition*, 19 July 2016

Comprehension

1 Outline the reasons why gun-carrying laws are a problem for the police.

2 Describe the measures suggested in the text that would lower the risk of fatal misunderstandings between police officers and gun-carrying citizens.

Analysis

3 Examine the author's point of view regarding gun bearing: Does he sympathize more with the police or with the people who carry legal firearms? Point to reasons for your assessment.

4 Compare the information in the text with *Crash*: Where in the film do handguns play an important role? What effect does easy access to firearms have on the lives of the characters in the film?

Beyond the Text

5 a Do some research on the right to own and carry a handgun in Germany.

b WRITING You discover a website that criticizes US gun laws and asks people in other countries to comment. Write a 250-word comment in which you compare the situations in the US and Germany and present your own opinion.

INFOBOX | Racial profiling

The accusation that the justice system in the US does not treat black and white people equally goes back as far as the Jim Crow era, in which segregation (i.e. the lawful separation of black and white Americans) and lynchings were present. It resurfaced in the 1980s and 1990s, when the deaths of black motorists stopped by white police officers for trivial traffic violations led to riots in American cities. Such incidents continued into the presidency of Barack Obama and led to accusations of racial profiling, meaning that people of colour are more often stopped by the police or are treated with less respect simply on the basis of their skin colour. The grassroots organization Black Lives Matter emerged in 2013 in response to repeated incidents of police injustice.

E2 RESPONDING TO DISCRIMINATION

1 **MEDIATION** Your American exchange partner, who belongs to an ethnic minority, asks you in an email how the German media have reported on the issue of racial profiling in the US. You find the following article by Fabian Wolff on the Internet and summarize the main points in English in an email reply for her/him.

Unser Leben zählt auch: *Black Lives Matter* FABIAN WOLFF

BLM, so die gängige Abkürzung, wurde vor genau drei Jahren geboren, am 13. Juli 2013. Als George Zimmerman in Florida des Mordes an Trayvon Martin freigesprochen wird, reagiert die Aktivistin Alicia Garza darauf mit einem Facebook-Post: Sie will ihren schwarzen Freunden versichern, dass
5 „unsere Leben etwas bedeuten". Zusammen mit Patrisse Cullors und Opal Tometi gründet sie die Organisation mit dem Hashtag #blacklivesmatter.

Dieser Slogan ist Selbstbehauptung, Selbstversicherung: Das eigene Leben ist mehr als die Angst, dass eine falsche Geste, ein falsches Wort in einer Begegnung mit der Polizei das Ende bedeuten kann. Er fasst das
10 Gefühl zusammen, mit der viele Mitglieder der afroamerikanischen Community, jedes einzelne mit einer individuellen Erfahrung von Schikane oder Gewalt, der Polizei begegnen. Der Hashtag wird in sozialen Medien sofort für die Verbreitung von Nachrichten über andere Fälle von Polizeigewalt und Ausgrenzung benutzt.

15 Ein Jahr nach der Gründung wird in Ferguson, Missouri, der 18-jährige Michael Brown mit sieben Schüssen von dem Polizisten Darren Wilson getötet. Es kommt zu Aufständen und Protesten. Mit einem *Freedom Ride*, in Anlehnung an die Bürgerrechtsaktivisten Freedom Riders, die in den Sechzigern mit Bussen durch die Südstaaten fuhren, wächst BLM von einer
20 Idee zu einer Bewegung. Im Chaos von Ferguson wird sie zur sichtbarsten und prominentesten Protestorganisation.

Mit geschicktem Einsatz sozialer Medien arbeitet BLM dafür, dass die Namen, Gesichter und Geschichten der von der Polizei getöteten Schwarzen nicht vergessen werden. Am 17. Juli 2014 wird der 43-jährige Eric Garner auf
25 Staten Island vom Polizisten Daniel Pantaleo wegen des Verkaufs loser Zigaretten 19 Sekunden lang im Würgegriff gehalten, ein Freund von Garner filmt das Geschehen. Seine letzten Worte „*I can't breathe*" macht BLM zu einem Slogan und zu einer Zustandsbeschreibung eines schwarzen Bewusstseins im permanenten Bedrohungszustand.

30 Auf Garner und Brown folgen Tamir Rice (12, Cleveland, zwei Schüsse in den Bauch wegen einer Spielzeugpistole), Laquan McDonald (17, Chicago, 16 Schüsse, neun davon in den Rücken), Sandra Bland (28, vermeintlicher Selbstmord in Haft nach einer Routineverkehrskontrolle), Walter Scott (50, North Charleston, fünf Schüsse), Tony Robinson (19, Madison, sieben
35 Schüsse). Viele dieser Opfer waren unbewaffnet. Es ist eine nicht abreißende Kette von Gewalttaten, die sonst nur als „Tragödien" diskutiert werden, um Ursachen zu überspielen. BLM justiert die Perspektive.

Bis heute hat die Organisation keine feste Struktur. Es gibt 30 Ortsgruppen, eine davon außerhalb der USA in Toronto. Die Gründerinnen gehören zu den prominentesten Gesichtern der Gruppe, sind aber keine Anführerinnen. [...] In der *Campaign Zero* entwerfen sie in zehn Punkten einen Plan, mit dem die Gewalt beendet und Respekt und Vertrauen hergestellt werden können: unabhängige Untersuchungen von Vorfällen polizeilicher Gewalt, De-Militarisierung der Polizei, bessere Ausbildung in Konfliktbewältigung. All diese Punkte drehen sich um das Grundkonzept: Die Polizei muss für ihr Handeln haftbar gemacht werden können.

Das ist ein simples, eigentlich noch nicht mal radikales demokratisches Prinzip, das in der Praxis immer wieder gebrochen wird. Weder Darren Wilson, der Michael Brown erschossen hat, noch Daniel Pantaleo, durch dessen Würgegriff Eric Garner gestorben ist, mussten sich vor Gericht verantworten. Augenzeugen, engagierte Staatsanwälte und Beteiligte, die sich in solchen Fällen für Gerechtigkeit einsetzen, erleben Repressalien und werden selbst angezeigt. Das ist das Polizeisystem, das BLM durchbrechen will. *Black Lives Matter* bedeutet nicht, dass etwa weiße Leben ohne Bedeutung sind. [...] Es ist stattdessen die einfache Einsicht, dass Schwarz-Sein in diesem System etwas mit Ausgrenzung zu tun hat.

From: 'Im Würgegriff des staatlichen Rassismus', *Zeit Online*, 13 July 2016

E3 ANALYSING A CARTOON

Comprehension

1 Describe the cartoon. What do you see and where? When and where is the cartoon set? Refer to the drawing on p. 48 in Part G if necessary.

Analysis

2 Explain the situation in the cartoon. What helps you understand the situation?

Beyond the Text

3 Relate the cartoon to the information you collected from Fabian Wolff's text and assess the effectiveness of the cartoon as a form of political commentary.

"I'll keep him covered...You radio Parking Violations and tell them we've got their man!"

PART E THE ISSUES BEHIND THE FILM

E4 RACE RELATIONS IN THE POST-OBAMA ERA SPT354801-02

When Barack Obama became the first African-American President of the United States in 2008, many Americans believed that the US had finally become a post-racial society (free of racism). Eight years later, *Washington Post* reporter Wesley Lowery takes a hard look at the state of the nation in an interview with NPR.

You will hear the interview twice. Before listening, take a look at the task below.

LISTENING While you are listening, write down the missing information to complete the sentences:

1 The title of Lowery's new book is _____.

2 According to Lowery, Obama was elected in 2008 on the belief that _____
_____.

3 Lowery says that Donald Trump appealed to voters who felt _____
_____.

4 Lowery refers to incidents of lynching during the Jim Crow era. The white people involved in the incidents complained that the media were only interested in the victims, not in _____
_____.

5 Lowery believes that all human beings have _____.

6 Lowery says that the debate today centres on the understanding of the term racism. On the one hand, there are people who say that racism means _____
_____.

On the other hand, there are those who say that any policy that leads to _____
_____ is racist.

7 Lowery says that during the past few years he has reported on _____ protests following police shootings.

8 At first, Lowery says, reporters made the mistake of concentrating on _____
_____.

A Black Lives Matter protest in New York City in 2016

PART F   EXAM PREPARATION – A SELF-TEST

1 Outline the most important information about each of the characters below. You need not write full sentences.

Graham Waters: _____
_____

Peter Waters: _____
_____

Anthony: _____
_____

Rick Cabot: _____
_____

Jean Cabot: _____
_____

Cameron Thayer: _____
_____

Christine Thayer: _____
_____

John Ryan: _____
_____

Tom Hansen: _____
_____

Daniel Ruiz: _____
_____

Farhad Golzari: _____
_____

PART F EXAM PREPARATION – A SELF-TEST

2 For each of the groups of characters named below, make notes on how they are connected with each other through the plot of the film *Crash*.

Ryan and Hansen	
Ryan and Christine	
Hansen and Cameron	
Hansen and Peter	
Cameron and Anthony	
Graham and Peter	
Graham and Rick Cabot	
Daniel and the Cabots	
Farhad and Daniel	
Anthony and the Cabots	
Anthony and the Korean man	

3 Choose one theme from the box below and explain in about 200 words how this theme is illustrated by the film.

loneliness   **prejudice**   **intolerance**

fear and suspicion   **race relations**   **pressure**

PART G   FILM STUDIES: EXTRAS

G1   SELECTED TERMS FOR FILM ANALYSIS

Camera range/kinds of shot	
close shot	In a **close shot** a person's face, shoulders and part of his/her arms are shown.
close-up	An entire human face from chin or lower neck to top of head fills the frame. Shows the finest nuances of expression.
extreme close-up	Parts of the face (or object) fill the entire frame.
medium shot	Characters and surroundings are shown at a moderate size, with characters seen from mid-body up. It is usually chosen to show one or two characters in action.
full shot	Includes the entire body of a character and not much else. The **full shot** is used to emphasize action and the constellation of characters.
long shot	Characters and surroundings are shown from a distance and in their entirety. It is usually used to introduce a new setting (see **establishing shot**) to show characters in relation to the action, to show movement over large distances, or to juxtapose different characters within one frame.

PART G   FILM STUDIES: EXTRAS

Camera perspective	
establishing shot	A **long shot** that establishes a setting, scene or mood; frequently used at the beginning of a scene.
over-the-shoulder shot	A shot taken with the camera placed behind a character who is only partially seen, looking over his/her shoulder. Usually used in dialogue scenes, showing the dialogue partner from the second character's point of view.
point-of-view shot	Also known as 'subjective camera'. A shot taken with the camera placed approximately where the character's eyes would be in order to depict a scene from the visual or emotional perspective of one of the characters.
shot / reverse shot **reverse-angle shot**	A **shot / reverse shot** is an **over-the-shoulder shot** followed by a **reverse-angle shot**. A **reverse-angle shot** is a shot in which the angle is opposite to that in the preceding shot.
Camera angle	
eye-level shot/ **straight-on angle**	A shot filmed at eye level.
high-angle shot	A shot filmed from above the object; may be used to diminish the character's importance.
low-angle shot	Filmed from below the object, a **low-angle shot** may be used to underline the importance or power of a character or object. Shown as a **point-of-view shot**, it indicates fear or respect on the part of the character 'viewing' a particular scene.

PART G FILM STUDIES: EXTRAS

Camera movement	
crane shot	A shot filmed from a crane that can move the camera in any direction. It is almost always linked to another movement of the camera, such as a **pan** or **tilt**, in which case it becomes a compound movement.
hand-held camera	A filming technique in which the camera is held by the operator during a take.
pan/panning shot	The camera moves horizontally from left to right or vice versa (**pan** right or **pan** left). A **panning shot** is often used to follow a character's movement or to indicate a **point-of-view shot** with the character looking around or searching for something.
tilt/tilt shot	The camera moves vertically upward or downward. A **tilt shot** is often used to indicate height or follow a character or object moving upwards or downwards, e.g. a leaf dropping.
tracking shot	Camera movement in which the entire camera is moved either forward, backward, laterally, or in a circular or irregular pattern. The camera is placed on a movable device (a camera dolly) moving along pre-laid tracks or is moved freely along a level surface (hand-held camera or steady cam). In a **tracking shot**, the camera range may either remain constant, following along next to or behind a moving character or object, or it may be used to get closer to or further away from the target object in a manner similar to a **zoom** shot. Usually used to indicate steady movement through the setting, e.g. indicating a character running or two characters walking together.
zoom	The stationary camera appears to approach a character or object by **zooming in** or to move farther away by **zooming out**.
Editing terms	
cross-cutting/ parallel action	Also known as parallel editing. An editing technique that alternates shots of two or more actions occurring in different places at the same time. Usually used to follow multiple plot lines, to compare or to juxtapose different actions or settings, or to show different reactions to a particular event.
cut	Transition from one shot to another. The most basic editing technique for connecting two shots within a scene and between scenes.
jump-cut	A (very) abrupt transition from one shot to another eleminating one strip of action and creating an effect of disorientation or rapid movement.

match cut	A technique in which two shots are linked by the same acting or by some form of visual parallelism. The two shots seem to continue uninterrupted, e.g. one door closing and then another door opening. **Match cuts** can be used to underline a connection between two separate elements. Often used to create a smooth flow between two scenes or, if using the same character in the action, to mark the passing of time.
dissolve	A transition between two shots created by gradually overlapping the last shot of a scene with the first shot of the next scene. This is done by superimposing a **fade-out** onto a **fade-in** of equal length. Often this transition is used to underline the connection between two scenes or to indicate a change of location or the passing of time.
fade-in **fade-out**	A transition between two shots. The last image of one scene gradually disappears from the screen (**fade-out**) to be replaced by a monochrome screen, and the first shot of the next scene gradually brightens from a blank screen to the whole image (**fade-in**). Often used to indicate a passing of time (e.g. from night to day), or to mark the beginning and end of a dream sequence (**flashback** or **flash-forward**).
flashback	A filmed sequence that goes back in narrative time to show events that took place earlier than the present-time of the film. Usually used to provide expository material and to underline the feelings and motives of characters.
flash-forward	A filmed sequence that moves forward in narrative time to show events that take place later than the present-time of the film. Usually used to underline the presence of an omniscient narrator, a **flash-forward** shows the consequences of a certain action that the characters are still unaware of. It gives the audience the impression of knowing more than the characters.
Additional film terms	
arc shot	Camera movement in which the entire camera moves around a subject or object in a circle.
backlighting	Filming a person or event against a background of light, e.g. the sun. It may produce an idealized, sometimes romantic effect.
camera operator	The person behind the camera(s); in major productions, the head of the camera team is usually called the **director of photography**.
cast	All actors who appear in a film.
clapboard (US)/ **clapperboard** (GB)	A small board which gives information about a film: e.g. the director, the director of photography, the scene, take number, date and time. It is filmed at the beginning of each **take**. It helps to identify all takes and cuts down continuity errors.

PART G FILM STUDIES: EXTRAS

credits	The list of people who were involved in the making of a film or television programme.
director	The person responsible for the artistic production of a film, involving all its creative elements, e.g. camerawork, editing, and the actors' interpretation of their roles.
director of photography	the head of the camera team
editor	(verb: edit) The person responsible for putting the camera shots together and arranging them into a finished product.
fade	Transition between two shots. The last image gradually disappears from the screen (**fade-out**) to be replaced by a monochrome screen, and the first shot of the next screen gradually brightens from a blank screen to the whole image (**fade-in**).
footage	A length of film made for TV or cinema.
frame	A single image of the film.
insert (shot)	A detail shot which quickly gives visual information necessary to understand the meaning of a scene, e.g. a newspaper page or a physical detail.
lighting	The creation of controlled illumination upon a scene or object to be filmed and thus the ultimate tool of the cinematographer. Light sources may be natural or artificial or both. If natural, the light may be directed onto the scene by reflecting devices. If artificial, it is of course aimed at the specific target area designated by the **director of photography** and channelled through the use of such devices as cookies, flags and doors. The light may also be diffused or it may be sharply focused. If, as might be said, cinematography is painting with light, lighting is the palette which the painter uses. Though methods for lighting a scene are highly varied, the one most commonly used in conventional practice is known as the 'Three-Point Lighting System'.
high-key lighting low-key lighting	The intensity and sharpness of light and corresponding shadow (or lack of this) which illuminates a scene is described as being either **high** or **low key**. This is true irrespective of whether the film is monochromatic or in colour. Lighting that creates comparatively little contrast between the light and dark areas of the shot is **high-key**, lighting that creates strong contrast between the light and dark areas of the shot is **low-key lighting**.
location	See: **set**.
mise-en-scène	Literally translated from French, the phrase means 'put upon the stage'; otherwise known simply as 'staging'. In film-making the term has come to mean the totality of how the director designs and sets in motion a given scene. All films use essentially the same techniques and processes. However, each individual film employs all of the variable elements of production provided by the technology available in its own distinct way. The elements generally used to define and analyse **mise-en-scène** are: setting, actor placement, actor movement, actor interpretation (ideally, but not always a collaboration between director and actor), camera movement, costumes and make-up.
motion picture/movie	US and Canadian terms for 'film'.

producer	The person responsible for the overall organization of a film or television production, especially the financing and marketing.
scene	A shot or series of shots that deal with a single action (see also **sequence**).
score	Film music.
screenplay	The script of a film or television show, usually including dialogue as well as rough descriptions of the setting, camera distance, camera movements, etc.
sequence	A part of a film dealing with one or more **scenes** that form a single continuous episode.
set	The site or location where a film is being shot.
shot	A single piece of film, however long or short, taken by a single camera without cuts.
soundtrack	The audio equivalent of the picture or image track, the **soundtrack** contains all the audio information which accompanies the film: dialogue, music, sound effects, etc.
still	A single photograph or screenshot from a film.
storyboard	A **storyboard** is a useful tool in the creation of any media production. It is a series of sketches or still photographs that show how the different shots might look when filmed. It almost looks like a comic book of the film.
take	A single attempt to film a shot. Though sometimes confused with **shot**, there can in fact be an unlimited number of takes of the same shot until either the director is satisfied or the producer calls a halt.
top shot	Extreme **high-angle shot** where the camera looks straight down.
voice-over	An off-screen voice that gives the audience necessary background information. It is often used in documentaries. In a narrative film, this technique often implies a first-person or omniscient narrator's point of view.
wipe	Transitional device in which shot B seemingly moves in either screen direction across shot A, thus effectively wiping off shot A and replacing it.

G2 WORKING WITH A FILM VIEWING LOG

You are probably used to keeping a reading log when studying a novel. When studying a film, it is even more important to take notes during the viewing process for future reference, as it is more difficult to go back to different parts of the film.

Before viewing
Find out all you can about the film you are going to see:

What genre does it belong to (e.g. feature film, documentary, video clip, newscast, commercial)? What country does it come from? When was it made? Are you going to see it in the original language (with or without subtitles), or is it a dubbed version? Was it made for television or for the cinema?

While viewing
Pay close attention to how visual and audio elements influence your reaction to the film:

- **Characters:** How does the film show you who the main characters are? What information do you get about them? What is their relationship to each other? What impression do they make on you, and why? Watch for facial expressions and body language that may convey important signals.

- **Setting:** How does the film let you know where the plot is set? What impression do you get of the setting? How do colour, music, lighting, background noise contribute to this impression?

- **Plot:** Is the plot introduced gradually (e.g. while the titles are being shown) or does the story begin in the middle and make the viewer draw conclusions based on indirect clues? Does it use flashbacks (or flash-forwards), or is the story told chronologically? Does the point of view of one character dominate, or does the film jump from one character to another? Is there one main plot, or does the film tell a series of loosely connected episodes? Are special effects used, and if so, to what effect?

- **Information:** Particularly in a documentary film, consider how the information is presented to the viewer. Does the director use music to appeal to the emotions and convince his/her audience? Is slow motion used? If so, when and why?

Using a viewing log can help you to keep track of what you notice while watching a film or video sequence.

Your viewing log might look like the following, but feel free to choose different categories to fit your own purposes:

What? (sequence/scene)	When/Where?	Who?	Filmic devices	Comments/Questions

After viewing

Go over your viewing log again and add information or comments. Think about your overall response to the film:

What emotions does the film arouse, and through what means? Do you identify with one or more of the characters, and if so, why? Does the film try to make you take sides, or does it encourage you to draw your own conclusions? Discuss these questions with others who have seen the film and analyse the reasons for your reactions. If possible, re-examine sequences/scenes that provoked conflicting views and discuss why you respond to them in different ways.

G3 HOW TO WRITE A FILM REVIEW

A film review is a written text that provides information about a film. It is intended either to recommend the film in question or to discourage people from seeing it. It can also help people to form their own opinion of the film.

- Start by considering the various elements which make up a film: the characters, the setting and the plot.
- Say what the film is about, giving the title, genre, name of the director and when it was made. Among other things, you may want to include awards and the names of actors.
- Give background information on the film and the director.
- Give specific information on what the film is about and provide a short summary without giving away the ending (unless this is explicitly required). You should aim to make your audience curious and encourage them to watch the film themselves rather than give everything away.
- Finish the review with your personal opinion (on the actors' performance or the adaptation of the novel, for instance), give reasons for your opinion and say whether you would recommend it or not.
- Remember to structure your review into three main parts:
  - an introduction with a catchy first sentence,
  - a main body outlining your main points (one per paragraph),
  - a conclusion summarizing the points made.

USEFUL VOCABULARY:

The film was produced/directed by …
It is set in / covers a period of / tells the story of …
The main characters are …
The story is rather weak/boring/unconvincing …
The storyline is entertaining/gripping/fascinating/clever …
I can thoroughly recommend the film.

G4 HOW TO ANALYSE FILM STILLS

When analysing a film still, concentrate on the following aspects:

- the content and setting of the still: what can be seen in the picture and where? When and where is the action set?

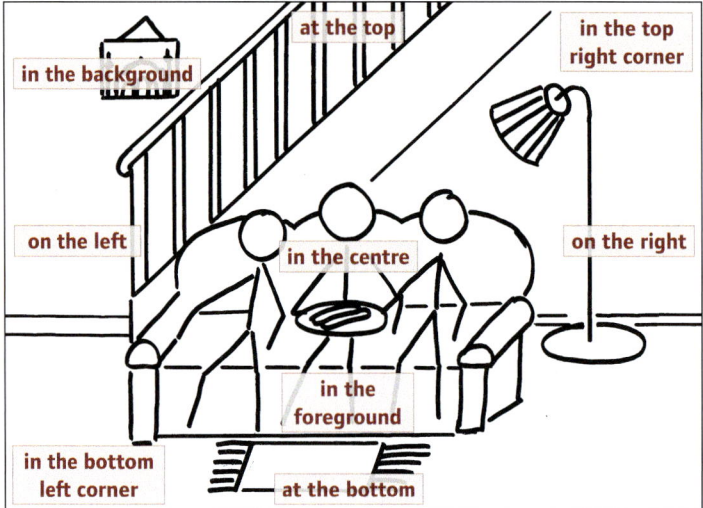

- the proportion of objects in the still; their arrangement in the foreground or background
- the camera angle and the perspective from which the still is taken
- the lighting and the colours of the still
- the overall impression: what impression is created by the above aspects?

USEFUL VOCABULARY:

The field size is a The camera takes a	long medium close …	shot	
The persons are The scene is …	filmed	from at	below above eye-level

1 Choose any still from the film and describe its major features to a partner. Make sure that your partner cannot see the original picture. Your partner draws a sketch while listening to your description. Then compare both pictures.